50
Reasons
to Love
ANIMALS

Frances Lincoln
Children's Books

Animals are amazing!

In this book, you can meet some of the incredible animals on planet Earth today, from blue whales to ancient sea turtles, gentle elephants to grizzly bears, and bold lions to colonies of penguins. Explore their homes, meet their neighbors, and discover how they have adapted to life on Earth.

These animals need our love more than ever before. Many of them are endangered, which means they are at risk of going extinct. Five times in Earth's history, over half of all animals and plants have mysteriously died out. But today, species are becoming extinct much faster than the natural rate. One of the biggest reasons why animals are disappearing is that humans are destroying the habitats where they live.

Discover 50 reasons to love the animals that
depend on wild places to survive. Find out why
these places are disappearing and how
you can help.

Dry savanna

This rich, grassy habitat is found near the equator, mostly in Africa. In the rainy season, giraffes, elephants, hippos, lions, wildebeest, and antelope wander over the land, visiting busy waterholes to drink. But many of these animals are threatened by hunting or habitat loss.

African elephant

1 Baby elephants take a year to figure out how to eat and drink with their strange, long noses.

trunk

2 Giraffes give birth standing up, so their babies start life with a bump as they fall to the ground!

giraffe

zebra

hippopotamus

3 Hippos keep their cool by releasing their own sunscreen, a sticky red fluid that protects them from the sun's harmful rays.

As dusk falls, predators like lions shake off their sleep and come out of the shadows to hunt. The roar of these magnificent beasts can be heard for miles but they are now extinct in many countries. The number of lions has almost halved in the last 20 years as people and their livestock have spread onto their wild land.

lion

4 Lions have special glow-in-the-dark orange eyes, which help them to spot prey in dim light.

lesser bushbaby

5 This noisy little primate folds its ear away when it leaps through tangled trees or falls asleep.

SHOW YOU LOVE A PANGOLIN

Pangolins are little known but very endangered animals. Discover 10 facts about pangolins and share them with your class at school.

6 The pangolin is a rare, shy creature that quickly curls into a scaly ball to escape predators like lions.

pangolin

In the day, elephants doze in the shade, or use their tusks to strip bark to eat. Once, there were ten million African elephants. Today, because of people using their land and poachers hunting their ivory tusks, there are fewer than 415,000 left. They share the savanna with ostriches and antelope, who are always ready to run for their lives to escape predators.

acacia tree

7 Some antelope don't seem to drink at all. They get enough water from the plants that they eat.

antelope

curved tusks

African elephants

secretary bird

 8 This bird can knock a dangerous puff adder or cobra on the head before swallowing it whole.

ostrich

stripped bark

SHOW YOU LOVE AN ELEPHANT

Ask if your school can celebrate World Elephant Day with art, stories, and poems to support organizations campaigning to save elephants.

Colorful coral reef

Coral reefs are made by tiny living polyps, which build hard tubes to protect their soft bodies. The reefs also provide food and shelter for more than a quarter of all plants and animals in the oceans. These "gardens of the sea" are home to an amazing variety of species, but they are being damaged by climate change.

hawksbill turtle

coral

9 Many marine sponges have chemicals that are used in medicine to treat diseases like cancer.

sponge

10 These jewels of the sea are actually fish, and strangely, the male seahorses give birth!

seahorse

green turtle

lobster

11 Spiny lobsters do the conga in long lines of 50 at a time, migrating across the seafloor!

Sea turtles have been swimming in our oceans for 100 million years. Some species visit coral reefs to feed as they travel thousands of miles back to the place they were born to lay their own eggs. But today they swim in polluted seas, get tangled in fishing nets, and feed in reefs damaged by climate change. All species of sea turtle are now endangered.

Kemp's ridley turtle

olive ridley turtle

12 Sea turtles mistake floating plastic bags for jellyfish, which multiply in warmer waters.

leatherback turtle

SHOW YOU LOVE A TURTLE

Learn about climate change! It's destroying coral reefs, which are dying as the sea warms up.

jellyfish

13 Sea turtles have to crawl further to lay their eggs out of reach of rising sea levels, caused by polar ice melting as Earth's temperature rises.

green turtle

blue-striped angelfish

hawksbill turtle

14 Coral polyps are home to tiny algae that give the corals their kaleidoscopic colors.

13

From slow-moving starfish and giant snails to graceful swimmers like sea turtles, dolphins, and sharks, many species are dependent on the sunlit waters of the coral reef. But as global warming increases the temperature of the oceans, coral reefs "bleach" and die. More than a quarter of coral reefs have disappeared in the past 30 years, threatening the survival of millions of creatures.

green turtle

15 Sea snakes help people study ocean currents, as they follow currents around the world.

tropical seas

sea snake

bottlenose dolphin

16 Dolphins find their food using sound waves, which bounce back from schools of fish.

school of sardines

reef shark

17 Reef sharks hang out in schools in the day but these top predators go solo for their nightly hunts.

Icy poles

For millions of years, bright white ice at the North and South Poles has reflected sunlight, helping to keep the planet cool. But today the Earth is getting hotter and the ice is melting fast. So the places where animals live are changing too. In the Arctic, polar bears are struggling to find ice strong enough for them to rest and fish.

polar bear

18 Did you know that polar bear skin is black under all that shaggy white fur?

19 Seals use their whiskers to help them hunt underwater, where they cannot smell.

seal pup

harp seal

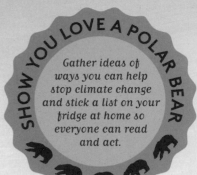

puffin

20 A puffin's beak changes color during the year, turning orange when it's looking for a mate.

killer whale

17

Emperor penguins live in Antarctica, which has the strongest winds, the driest desert, and the lowest temperatures on the planet. But the ice here is disappearing, fast. If this continues, some scientists believe that half of all emperor penguins could disappear in the next 50 years.

ice

21 Emperor penguins can survive in very low temperatures of -76 degrees Fahrenheit. Brrrr!

emperor penguins

22 Unlike other birds, penguins have solid bones. This makes them heavy and helps them to dive deep.

chicks

23 Antarctic seal pup fur keeps them cozy and warm in freezing Antarctic air.

seal pup

Blue whales migrate from the poles to tropical waters, where they mate and, months later, give birth to the biggest babies in the world. Like other great whales, this astonishingly large mammal almost died out during the 20th century because of humans hunting for its meat, oil and bones. Many whales are still endangered today.

sea ice

blue whale calf

24 Tiny algae grow on blue whales' super-slippery bellies, so they look yellow from below and bright blue from above.

SHOW YOU LOVE A WHALE

Start campaigning! Ask your school to write to the Japanese, Icelandic, and Norwegian embassies asking them to stop whaling.

25 Killer whales belong to the same family as dolphins, not whales.

killer whale

blue whale

Steller's jay

26 Bears dance and scratch against trees to leave a scent for other bears to find.

black bear

27 Porcupines can climb trees to look for food and even build nests in the branches.

porcupine

Evergreen forest

Forests are the lungs of our planet, and home to most animals and plants on land. Some evergreen forests are peaceful but others are noisy with machines cutting down trees for timber and paper, for people all over the world.

SHOW YOU LOVE A BEAR

People live peacefully alongside wild animals by understanding their behavior. Find out how bears behave with their cubs.

28 Pine martens chat to their mates in huffs, chuckles, and screams.

cub

Bamboo forest grows fast, providing food for animals like pandas that rely on it to survive. But people are dividing up the forest with roads, which makes it harder for pandas to meet and mate. More bamboo is also being cut down for paper, furniture and farms as the human population increases. Pandas are endangered, but projects to save pandas are helping panda populations grow.

giant panda

29 Bamboo has few nutrients, so although pandas chew it all day, they still have little energy to move.

30 Snub-nosed monkeys live in the coldest, highest places of any monkey on Earth.

snub-nosed monkey

golden pheasant

31 The bright feathers of these beautiful birds fade in the sun, so they hide in shadowy forests.

bamboo

Grizzly bears like to live in old forests, close to rivers and streams. But this habitat is under threat as people cut down trees to build roads in their search for oil and gas. Unfortunately, this can pollute the cool mountain rivers, threatening freshwater as well as forest animals. New roads are a danger to grizzlies too, which today occupy only a tiny bit of the land they used to roam.

32 Grizzly bears look clumsy and slow but they can run as fast as a race horse!

cubs

grizzly bear

33 Bears sometimes catch salmon and elk, but mostly they just eat berries, leaves, and nuts.

34 An elk's velvety antlers grow more if the sun shines.

elk

lake

horsetail plant

27

Open ocean

Ocean covers most of our great blue planet. It is full of life—even on the deep seabed there are bizarre creatures in unexplored habitats—and we rely on its salty waters for food.

deep ocean

octopus

35 Octopuses are super smart. They solve problems, use tools and, if bored, they play!

But all kinds of marine life, from the sunlit surface right down to the seabed, can get tangled in fishing nets as ships trawl for fish in the open seas.

36 Even the biggest animal on Earth, the blue whale, is difficult to find in the wide, open seas.

blue whale

seabed

Penguins, seals, and whales feast in the cold waters of the Southern Ocean. Many animals here eat krill, but this tiny pink creature is becoming harder to find. Young krill rely on sea ice for shelter and food, so the loss of sea ice due to climate change could lead to lower numbers of krill. This may threaten the future of many animals in the Antarctic food chain.

gentoo penguins

37 Gentoo penguins are busy feeders, making up to 450 dives each day!

leopard seal

38 The only predator of the gigantic, blubbery leopard seal is the deadly killer whale.

39 The longest penguin dive ever recorded was for 32 minutes, by an Emperor penguin.

bubbles

mackerel icefish

Only a tiny part of the ocean is protected. Around the world, oceans are polluted—awash with plastic—and overfished. Scientists estimate that the population of ocean animals has halved over the last 40 years. But many countries are working together to create more protected areas and to care for different ocean habitats.

fishing boat

40 Dolphins are deep thinkers— the emotional part of their brain may be more complicated than ours.

dolphins

seal

42 Pelicans have giant throat pouches that they fill with water and swing around to keep cool.

whale fluke

pelican

41 From the tip of its fluke all the way to its gigantic mouth, the blue whale is the biggest animal on Earth.

Tropical forest

Tropical forests are warm, tangled jungles, home to half the species on Earth. From parrots squawking in the canopy to monkeys swinging between branches, elephants ambling and armies of ants scurrying across the forest floor, rain forests explode with life.

scratching stick

 43 Elephants solve problems by using tools like sticks to scratch and branches to swat at flies.

One of the biggest threats to this habitat is illegal logging (cutting down trees), which is destroying the places where forest animals live.

orangutan

45 Orangutans are forest gardeners. They eat fruit and have hundreds of seeds in their poop, which gets scattered as they travel.

Bengal tiger

44 You can tell a tiger by its stripes. Each tiger is unique, just like your fingerprints.

fly swatter branch

Asian elephants

Local people as well as wildlife depend on forests for their homes, lives and food. Southeast Asia is a land of forests but many are now threatened by palm oil plantations. Companies are cutting down trees to plant this crop for people all over the world. So sun bears, orangutans and other animals are having to live in smaller and smaller areas of forest land.

SHOW YOU LOVE A SUN BEAR

From food to toothpaste, palm oil is widely used — look out for better options such as sustainable palm oil or palm oil-free products in stores.

sun bear

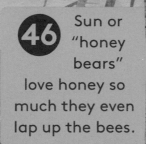

46 Sun or "honey bears" love honey so much they even lap up the bees.

hive

nest

hornbill

47 Hornbills are the only birds with eyelashes, protecting their eyes from dust and sun.

African pear tree

48 Chimpanzees are more closely related to humans than gorillas.

western lowland gorillas

SHOW YOU LOVE AN ELEPHANT

Discover some surprising ways that farmers are encouraging elephants away from their crops—with a hum and a sticky reward. ("Buzzzzz" is a clue!)

African forest elephant

Elephants roam forests in West Africa, often sharing spaces with people and sometimes even gorillas. But a third of all lowland gorillas have been killed by Ebola, a fast-spreading, deadly disease that people catch too. Gorillas also face illegal poaching by local people for their meat.

great blue turaco

49 The blue turaco climbs up high to avoid hunters after its bright blue and yellow feathers, sought for headdresses used in ceremonies.

50 Elephants are difficult to find among the trees. If you are counting forest elephants, their poop is often the only clue.

poo

Brimming with creative inspiration, how-to projects, and useful information to enrich your everyday life, Quarto Knows is a favorite destination for those pursuing their interests and passions. Visit our site and dig deeper with our books into your area of interest: Quarto Creates, Quarto Cooks, Quarto Homes, Quarto Lives, Quarto Drives, Quarto Explores, Quarto Gifts, or Quarto Kids.

Inspiring | Educating | Creating | Entertaining

This omnibus edition first published in 2020 by Frances Lincoln Children's Books, an imprint of The Quarto Group.
The Old Brewery, 6 Blundell Street, London N7 9BH, United Kingdom.
T (0)20 7700 6700 F (0)20 7700 8066 **www.QuartoKnows.com**

Published in association with the Natural History Museum

A catalog record for this book is available from the British Library.

ISBN 978-0-7112-5246-2

The illustrations were created digitally
Set in BrownPro

Published by Katie Cotton
Designed by Sasha Moxon
Edited by Katy Flint
Production by Caragh McAleenan

Manufactured in China 122019
1 3 5 7 9 8 6 4 2

FSC
www.fsc.org
MIX
Paper from responsible sources
FSC® C016973